Our Exciting Earth!

CAVES

By Tanner Billings

Gareth Stevens
PUBLISHING

Please visit our website, www.garethstevens.com.
For a free color catalog of all our high-quality books, call toll free 1-800-542-2595 or fax 1-877-542-2596.

Library of Congress Cataloging-in-Publication Data

Names: Billings, Tanner, author.
Title: Caves / Tanner Billings.
Description: New York : Gareth Stevens Publishing, [2023] | Series: Our exciting earth! | Includes index.
Identifiers: LCCN 2021039103 | ISBN 9781538275641 (Set) | ISBN 9781538275658 (Library Binding) | ISBN 9781538275634 (Paperback) | ISBN 9781538275665 (eBook)
Subjects: LCSH: Caves–Juvenile literature.
Classification: LCC GB601.2 .B5 2023 | DDC 551.44/7–dc23
LC record available at https://lccn.loc.gov/2021039103

Published in 2023 by
Gareth Stevens Publishing
29 East 21st Street
New York, NY 10010

Editor: Kate Mikoley
Designer: Tanya Dellaccio

Photo credits: Cover Balate Dorin/Shutterstock.com; p. 5 kid315/Shutterstock.com; p. 7 triocean/Shutterstock.com; p. 9 Double Bind Photography/Shutterstock.com; p. 11 fotofundi/Shutterstock.com; p. 13 Ian Crocker/Shutterstock.com; p. 15 aquapix/Shutterstock.com; p. 17 Kuznetsova Julia/Shutterstock.com; p. 19 Dirk Daniel Mann/Shutterstock.com; p. 21 keywordphil/Shutterstock.com; p. 23 Dmitry Pichugin/Shutterstock.com.

Printed in the United States of America

CPSIA compliance information: Batch #CSGS23: For further information contact Gareth Stevens, New York, New York at 1-800-542-2595.

Contents

Cool Caves 4

Where Are Caves? 10

Life in Caves 20

Words to Know 24

Index. 24

A cave is a big hole.
It is made by nature.

Most are made of rock.
Many are limestone.

Water cuts a hole
in the rock.
This makes the cave.

A cave can be
in the ground.

It can be on the side of a hill.

Some are in water.

Some are made of ice.

Caves can be long. Some have many twists and turns.

Bats live in caves. They come out at night to eat.

People used to live
in caves.
Some drew on walls.

Words to Know

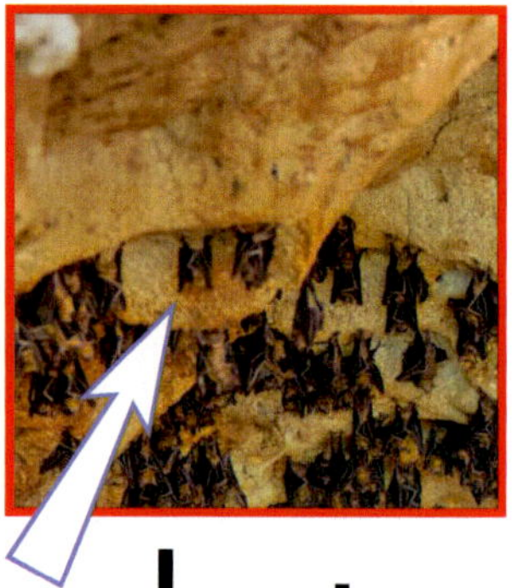

bat

hill

water

Index

bats 20

hills 12

ice 16

limestone 6